From Beginning To End

TERESA CARRISOZA

Edited by Ruth Federico

Rfederico2000@aol.com

ISBN: 0615987222
ISBN-13: 978-0615987224

DEDICATION

I dedicate this book to my children Tammy, Chipper, Michelle, Tomas, Teresa, Lorenzo, Charee, and Chris.

My guys from the lighthouse who loved me as a real mom.
I also want to thank my adopted sister Terri who knew I was more than I thought I would be. She put me through college, and she kept telling me that I would make it through to the end.

My adopted Mom Aimee who has gone to be with the Lord, to my adopted Dad Pat who has gone to be with the Lord and was so good to my children and me.

To the guys from the Lighthouse who are still like family, and call me Mama Tracy. Loto, Rene, Richard. Lupe, Sulu, and my daughter in love Pati.

There are people who have come through my life but these have stayed. The ones I have mentioned I will pray for daily. Bless you all.

CONTENTS

THE BEGINNING

Their marriage was doomed from the start. They had been married two years ago, and, already, the problems were at the boiling point.

It was September 16, 1953 at 1:00 am in the morning, on a hot Indian summer night. Jose Diaz nervously paced the waiting room at St. Mary's Hospital. Everything in that hospital was white and sterile. The nurses scurried down the halls in their white starched uniforms. Even the TVs in the rooms were white.

His dark wavy hair was combed to the side. Women couldn't help falling in love with those dark brown eyes. He wore a gray suit and a white button down shirt. He had dusted off his black loafers and shined the penny in each of them.

Genevieve, his wife, was in labor with his first child. She wore her long red curly hair in a ponytail. Her eyes were as blue as the ocean in Hawaii. This would be her second child; she was not nervous.

They didn't speak. They sat thinking. He thought about how long it would take to be over. Would it be a boy or a girl? Would it look like his side or hers? Genevieve's thoughts were on how this baby could save their marriage.

Jose's family did not approve of Genevieve. She had been divorced and had a five- year- old daughter named Martha. When they found out about her, Jose's brother Abel came to talk to him before the wedding. He explained that the family was not prejudiced, but she had been with a man before, and she was not even Spanish. But all Jose could see were her ocean blue eyes, fire-red hair, and her five-foot-two petite body. At that time, he felt nothing could destroy their love for each other.

"It's a girl", the nurse said as she rushed past him to take the baby to the nursery. Tracy weighed 9 lbs. three ounces. Born with a full head of black wavy hair. She didn't look like either one of them.

Jose called his parents from the lobby phone so Genevieve could rest. His brother Juan was at their parents' home waiting for the call. They would love this baby because it was Jose's, even if they didn't approve of his choice for a wife.

"It's a big healthy girl," Jose said before saying "Hi" to the one who answered the phone. "She has a lot of wavy hair like mine," he told his brother Juan who had answered the parents phone.

"Congratulations, *Hermano*."

Juan told everyone at his parents' house who had gathered waiting for the news. Then his mom was on the phone talking, asking all the questions women always ask. Jose kept putting dimes in the pay phone every time the operator would ask for more money for more minutes to talk.

The weeks went fast; the new baby girl and mom were home. Jose did not expect the night crying from the colic that Tracy developed. The tiredness from the second job also did not help him sleep. The tension in the house grew and grew. The baby that Genevieve thought would bring Jose and her closer put an even greater strain on their marriage. Genevieve took a few drinks to help calm her brittle nerves and get some sleep. Then she took a few more.

When Jose was home, Genevieve slept. He made Tracy's bottles and changed her diapers. She did not cry as much when he held her. When the family came to see the baby, Genevieve stayed in her room and did not come out for any reason.

She would make remarks to herself when they would be speaking to each other in Spanish.

"Blah, blah, blah, this is America. They need to speak English or go back where they came from". She resented them more every day. She knew they did not like them, but she couldn't say anything about them coming to see their grandchild. Sometimes she wished they would not come over at all.

Before the baby was born, they never came over. She never went with Jose to visit them. He took Martha and they always acted as if they were glad to see her. They taught her Spanish and they would even talk in broken English to her. But when Genevieve was there, they only spoke Spanish, and Jose would tell her what they were saying.

At least once a month the Diaz's would pile up in the old black Hudson and drive from New York to New Jersey to see Tracy and bring her gifts. Of course, they always brought Martha something also. They were close to her and loved her as if she was their granddaughter.

By the time Tracy was six months old, Genevieve started drinking more then she should. The emotional pain from in-laws and Tracy's colic started taking their toll.

One March afternoon, Genevieve was thinking and drinking a little too much, when the thought entered her mind, "If I didn't have Tracy, I could take Martha and leave." Genevieve knew that Jose's family would never let her leave and take Tracy. The drinking increased. Tracy's crying got worse until Genevieve, in a drunken daze, let her cigarette fall from her hand to the carpet. She reached for the can of lighter fluid. She walked down the hall to Tracy's carpet outside her door, and squirted the area all the way, to where the cigarette laid.

As she watched the carpet smolder, she could still hear Tracy crying. In her drunken, depressed state, she felt this fire would end the depression she had. She felt she would be able to leave Jose and his interfering family. Genevieve could remember the looks the family always gave her when Jose was not looking. They insisted on speaking in Spanish even though they knew she did not understand the language.

"When this is over I won't care what they say in Spanish" Genevieve reached for another can of beer and waited.

A small flame started down the hall that led to the room where Tracy was still crying. When she was sure the fire was going toward Tracy's room and not die out, she slowly walked out the trailer door and sat outside waiting for the fire to end her problems. Within a few minutes, she passed out drunk.

Moments later, Tracy's seven-year-old sister, Martha came home from school. Martha was a thin child with long blond hair. She wore a thick jacket, snow pants and red boots. She clipped her gloves to her jacket. It was easier to carry her books with the gloves off. She did not have the hood from her jacket on she had a red hat with a pompom on the top.

Smoke poured out of the trailer windows. Her mother slept in a chair on the small porch just outside the trailer door. Her baby sister was nowhere in sight. She ran into the trailer and found the door to Tracy's room in flames. Smoke poured out the open door causing Martha to cough uncontrollably. Her eyes watered making it difficult to see clearly. Thinking that the trailer window to Tracy's room might be unlocked, Martha ran to the back of the trailer, climbed on top of an old wringer washer. She climbed inside to Tracy's crib. Martha knew she had to work fast before the smoke overcame her. She saw Tracy's body just lying in her crib. She hoped the baby was not dead.

Tracy was not crying and her color was off. Martha threw a quilt out the window on the top of the washer; next, she threw Tracy's snowsuit out to pad her fall. Each time she went to the window, she took a deep breath of clean air. Finally, she put Tracy out the window.

"I'll wrap her up after I get her outside," she thought. After they were both safely out, Martha wrapped her sister in the quilt, picked up the snow suit, and ran to see if any neighbors were home. Martha went to three trailers before she found someone. By that time, the baby's coloring was better, and she was crying and coughing, again.

Martha knocked hard on the neighbor's door. When Mrs. Jones door opened, Martha cried, "Our trailer's on fire! Call the fire department!"

"Yes come in, I'll call now!" Mrs. Jones led them inside.

After calling the fire department, Mrs. Jones warmed a bottle of milk she had from her baby and fed it to Tracy.

"Where are your mom and dad?" she asked Martha.

Martha couldn't bring herself to say that her mother passed out drunk in a chair outside their trailer. So she lied, "My mom went to pick up my dad from work, and I tried to put my mom's cigarette out and the rug caught on fire."

Martha talked fast and nervously crying.

"Its O.K. accidents happen," Mrs. Jones, told her, trying to ease what she thought was guilt.

The fire department responded quickly. By then Tracy was asleep on the neighbor's couch. Martha asked if she could leave her sister there while she checked to see if her parents were home. The neighbor said, "O.K. but don't get in the way."

When Martha got to the trailer, her mother was awake and screaming, "My baby, save my baby!"

Martha knew in her heart her mother did not care if they saved her baby or not; and she was just putting on an act for those around. Martha waited and watched till she saw her step-father drive up, then she slowly walked over to the fireman who was giving orders, and told him, "My baby sister is not in that trailer. She is in Mrs. Jones trailer." She pointed to the trailer her sister was in. "I came home and found my sister in the trailer with fire all over the door; I climbed in the back window and got her out."

"Where were your parents?" The man asked.

"I don't know," Martha answered and followed the paramedic to where Tracy was sleeping. They took Tracy away in the ambulance to check her lungs. She heard the other man tell her parents where Tracy and Martha were. She also heard him asking her parent many questions.

Too bad, the baby could not tell what really happened. Too bad, Martha could not tell what really happened. Fear was a major part of this family.

The fire department decided the fire was an accident. Martha wished she had told the truth to everyone. Maybe her mom would have had to stop drinking. She hated feeling she always had to protect the family. The family stayed in a motel until they were able to buy a four-bedroom house. The fire scared Genevieve and her drinking slowed down. However, life for Tracy only got worse after they moved into the new house..

TRACY LEARNS TO BE QUIET

Jose bought a green house on Mansfield drive in Fair Lawn New Jersey. It had two bedrooms, one bathroom, kitchen and living room down stairs. Upstairs there were two more bedrooms and a full bathroom. There was also a big finished basement. One side was the workshop where Jose worked on things. On the wall was a big picture of the ship that he was on in World War II. He was so proud of that picture and always had a story to tell the girls about life on the ship at sea. He told how he joined the Navy.

He had gone to the post office alone to register for his citizen papers since he was born in Spain. He went into the wrong office. He did not let the people know he did not speak English so he kept saying "yes" to whatever they asked. Finally, they pointed down to a paper and, as they tapped at the paper, he figured they wanted him to sign his name.

He signed his name and a month later two Navy police came to his parents' house asking for him. They brought a Spanish-speaking person who explained in their own language that Jose had joined the navy. The family was surprised but could do nothing. One of the Navy police told Jose, "Get your tooth brush. You're in the navy now." With that, Jose kissed his mom goodbye and left with the men.

In the work area Jose had his tools where he did work and fixed things around the house if they broke. He also made things with the router and wood saw. He fixed Martha's bike that Genevieve had driven over when it was by the driveway. No one knew if she drove over it going in or out of the driveway.

The other half they called the playroom TV room. That is where the girls watched the Little Rascals and Mickey Mouse before going to school.

On the other side of the staircase, was the freezer and a sewing room, a request from Genevieve, even though she was never down there. The other half had the washer and dryer, and mangle for pressing cloths. It look something like a tanning bed of today, but it was for pressing cloths.

The back yard was fenced in and Jose planted two weeping willow trees - one on each side of the yard. All you could see for miles was a wooded area. Jose put a metal swing set for the girls to play. There was a concrete patio with a metal awning. When it rained, you could hear it hitting the awning before you could see it outside. There was no grass in the back, but there was in the front yard. A two-car garage was also attached to the house with a door that went into the hallway of the inside of the house. But it was not a home just a house. A home should be filled with love and laughter. This house was filled with anger and name-calling.

Tracy learned early not to depend on her Mom and Dad. She grew to be a very quiet, scared and abused child. Her sister Martha took care of her most of the time when she was not in school. In the morning, Martha made her breakfast, and put her in the playpen, fixed her a bottle of milk, and went to school. She stayed in the same diaper with only one bottle until Martha came home from school for lunch. Tracy knew from the time she was a year old that crying would only cause her punishment.

Tracy's mother, Genevieve, stayed in bed until eleven. She didn't care what was happening to Tracy. When Genevieve would first wake up, she would go straight to the kitchen to drink a lot of coffee in order to make the way she felt from drinking too much the night before go away. She didn't wash her face or fix her hair. She just walked from her bed to the kitchen where the coffee pot was.

Tracy's father, Jose was so busy working two jobs he was hardly ever home, (or perhaps he did not want to be.) He worked for the Sheriff Department during the night. He also worked his second Job at Benedict Aviation Plant mornings. Martha was the only one who made time for Tracy.

After lunch, Martha changed Tracy's diaper and wet clothes, made her lunch, gave her another bottle, put her back in the playpen, and went back to school. Tracy never cried when Martha left. She knew better than to let her mother hear her cry.

Martha took care of Tracy after school too. She did not dare go to a friend's house or stay after school for sports. She had to take care of Tracy. She fed her dinner, gave her a bath, and put Tracy to sleep in her bed so she could do her homework. Martha slept with her at night. She made her a bottle at night when Tracy woke up at night. However, as time passed and Tracy was getting older things got worse for her. Tracy no longer cried. She no longer laughed. She was like a rag doll, not like other babies her age.

Genevieve appeared to be a warm, loving, sober person around outsiders. However, at home, alone, she was always on edge. She did the best she knew how to hide the pain that took over her mind and body. The drinking took over her life, and the lives of all who were around her. She was in denial of the effect her drinking was having on the whole family. One never spoke to Genevieve until after her second or third cup of coffee. Moments after people left and Genevieve was alone she ran for a beer or some kind of alcoholic drink. She shook all over until the liquor started to take effect.

Drinking became more important than anyone or anything. It even controlled her thinking. There were days when she was so sick of herself she would swear she would never drink again. However, she would never admit it controlled her. The days on which Genevieve tried to stop drinking were scary for Tracy. Genevieve became a monster. On those days, Tracy just stayed out of Genevieve's sight. Tracy knew not to cry or ask for anything.

Sometimes Tracy did not want Genevieve to stop drinking. When Genevieve was drunk Tracy knew things would not get that bad for her. Martha would play with her after school. Until then Tracy played in her hiding places behind the sofa or under Martha's bed. Genevieve was drinking and forgot anyone was around. There was just her and her drinking. If she did see Tracy, Genevieve just yelled at her and told Tracy things like, "Get out of here or I'll lock you in the hall closet till you die," or "I wish I never had you! Go away!"

However, she did not come after Tracy to hurt her or lock her in the hall closet. Tracy just had to stay out of her way until Genevieve was asleep or passed out from her drinking.

Jose cooked dinner and went to his second job. After Martha fed and bathed her, they watched TV in Jose's bedroom upstairs. Genevieve's bedroom had always been downstairs as far back as Tracy could remember. Jose told Martha he slept upstairs because their mom drank too much. In addition, the whole room smelled like rotten beer.

Tracy bedroom was down stairs across the hall from her parent's bedroom, but she never slept there anymore. She was afraid Genevieve would hurt her if she slept there. She liked sleeping with her sister Martha in the big bed.

Tracy liked this time; Martha made her laugh. She always felt loved when she was with Martha. Martha tickled her and rocked her to sleep in grandmother's rocker.

However, on the days Genevieve was trying to stop drinking, it was a horror for Tracy. Genevieve would tell Tracy she chewed too loudly, or that she was yelling when she was only talking to her doll. Genevieve accused her of anything just to hit Tracy and throw her in the closet. Then Genevieve would go sit outside so she could not hear Tracy screaming and crying. Genevieve put Tracy in the hall closet and looked for something to drink. After all, it was Tracy's fault she started drinking again. She knew Martha would take her off her hands when she got home from school.

The closet was in the entryway of the front of the house. It was for coats to hang in the winter. It was small to start with, yet when the coats were in it, it was smaller. There was a light with a chain hanging in the middle of the ceiling, but Tracy was never tall enough to reach it. Therefore, Tracy was in the dark until Martha came and opened the door.

Tracy hated the sound of the back door closing because that meant Genevieve had gone out back to get a Weeping Willow branch from the tree outside. No matter where she ran and hid, her mom would always find her. Then she would scream at Tracy and whip her with the tree branch until broke. Weeping willow branches took a long time to break. The welts on Tracy body were like lines on a map going in different directions. Blood oozed from the welts, but this did not matter to Genevieve.

When the switch broke, Genevieve took Tracy by the arm, throw her into the hall closet, and lock Tracy in the dark. Sometimes when Genevieve put her in the closet Tracy was barely conscious.

"I'm sorry mama, I'll be good. I won't do it again." Tracy pleaded repeatedly.

However, Genevieve just laughed. "If I have to suffer you have to suffer." The beatings continued until Tracy did not cry or make a sound anymore. Sometimes she passed out before the willow branch broke. Genevieve picked up her limp body and threw her in the hall closet. Genevieve was unable to love this child. She only saw Tracy as the reason she drank and was unhappy.

Sometimes it seemed that Martha took long time coming home, but Tracy knew her sister would get her out of the closet.

Genevieve always told Martha, "That stupid kid locked herself in the closet. She knew she couldn't get out from there."

They both knew it was a lie. The latch was on the outside of the door. On those days, Martha took Tracy upstairs gave her a bath and tried to comfort her. The dried blood took forever to come off. Then she put medicine on the open wounds. Sometimes Tracy whimpered, but nothing would break the spell the closet had on her. Sometimes Tracy thought she was dreaming, and that Martha was talking to her. But Martha's voice sounded so far away.

Sometimes Martha got scared and cried because Tracy said and did nothing. There was nowhere to turn. Martha was afraid Tracy would die in her bed. Martha was a child herself; she wasn't prepared for this.

Sometime Tracy just stared blankly and trembled. Whenever Tracy staring and trembling lasted for a long time, Martha would be so scared, she would begin to pray to Jesus to help her help Tracy.

When Jose came home at night late at night after working two jobs Jose would look in on the girls with pain in his eyes, shake his head, go downstairs and yell at Genevieve. Jose felt helpless to do anything for the girls. He felt angry with himself for not doing anything to stop the madness. Then he would go to work, and Genevieve would start drinking again.

Weekends and summers were better; Martha and Tracy spent those times with Jose's parents. Friday, granddad picked them up, and Sunday night he brought them back home. Unless it was summer, then they stayed until it was a week before school started. It was so much better there. No yelling, only love and feeling safe.

Tracy and Martha loved it at their grandparents. They visited the zoo or went to the Atlantic Ocean. Yet, every time they went back home, Tracy started crying. She knew she could cry in granddad' s car, and no one would hit or hurt her. Just knowing they were going back home to Genevieve triggered fear and panic in Tracy. Sometimes, she even cried while granddad was at the house. However, when he would start to leave the crying would stop and Martha would take her up stairs to their bedroom.

How long could this go on before it reached the boiling point? Only God knew. However, for a few months, during the summer, they could put the madness on hold and live a somewhat normal life.

WHERE DO YOU GO FOR PEACE?

Summer was over, and Tracy was ready to start school. Tracy and Martha hated coming home from Granddad's. Jose gave grandma the money to buy their school clothes. There were many pretty dresses, black patent leather shoes, socks and underwear; the works.

However, this summer Tracy was no longer the playful little girl she always became at granddads. This year was different. No matter what anyone asked, her she answered, "If you want to" or "I don't care, whatever you want to do." There was an empty look in her eyes. No smiles, no laughing, just sadness.

Tracy's grandparents didn't know what was wrong with her, but Martha knew. Genevieve had tried more often to stop drinking that year. That meant more time in the hall closet this year. Jose gave Genevieve an ultimatum to stop drinking, or he was taking the girls and leaving her. But Genevieve hurt Tracy more than ever. She hit her with anything she could get her hands on. She used belts, extension cords, anything in reach. Martha wanted to tell someone to make the pain and suffering stop, but she was afraid no one would believe her. Maybe with Tracy going to school things would be different; Martha hoped and prayed silently every night for God to stop the nightmare she and Tracy were living.

The first day of school, Martha rushed home at lunch to take Tracy to her afternoon kindergarten class. When the teacher asked Martha why she and not her mother had brought Tracy to school, Martha lied.

"My mother has polio; she's at home with a nurse. The nurse watches Mom and Tracy. So, I volunteered to take her and bring her home," she explained.

The teacher Miss Medina said no more and poor twelve-year-old

Martha went back to her class. The lies were being more farfetched. This lie was not planned it just came off the top of her head. Miss Medina was a young woman about 25 years old. This was her first teaching position. She was tall, about five foot seven, with long black hair she wore in a bun on the top of her head. She had in wire glasses on and very red lipstick. She always wore a blouse with ruffles around her collar and long pant with black shoes. She was not pretty but she was not ugly, she was nice looking. She always spoke in a soft voice.

After school, Tracy waited for Martha to come get her from class. They walked home in silence; they were worried about their mother's condition. Would Genevieve be drunk or sober? If she was awake and drunk, they could not go home. If she passed out, they could go upstairs until Dad came home. Martha always made Tracy wait three houses down from their house so she could look in the window and check on what Mom was doing. If Genevieve was asleep, she took Tracy home. If she was awake, Martha got the sandwiches she always hid in the bushes beside the house.

Before Martha left for school in the morning, she would make peanut butter and jelly sandwiches, wrap them in foil and hid them in the bushes. She told Tracy "If mom starts to get crazy, run out side and hid in the bushes till I get there". If Genevieve was awake, they would take the hidden sandwiches and go to the park until after dad came home.

In January, the teacher sent a note home with Tracy for her parents. Martha worried what the note said. She had to read it and find out. Today, Martha just got the sandwiches and they went to the park. Martha read the letter:

Dear Mr. and Mrs. Diaz,

This letter is to inform you of
your daughter, Tracy's progress
for the first quarter,

Tracy does not seem to be absorbing
much of what we are teaching. If this
continues, I will be forced to have her
repeat this class next year or we might
have to look at Special Ed as an option.

I hope this will improve so we do not
have to take these steps.

Thank you
Miss Medina

Martha was relieved. She worried the teacher might want Genevieve for a conference, or that the teacher wanted to come to the house for a conference. Thank God, she did not want to meet with them; this meant the teacher still believed Genevieve was too sick to come to school.

However, the lying made Martha nervous. What If Genevieve came to the school, either drunk or sober? What if she, Martha, got sick and was unable to bring Tracy to school? How was she going to keep Tracy and Genevieve apart?

This was too much for any child twelve years old. Next year she went to junior high school. Even though the school was next to Tracy's, Martha did not know what her hours would be.

"Oh God, help me find a way," Martha said to herself as she left the park to take Tracy home. Martha started to cry as she walked towards home with Tracy following behind her.

"I am too young to worry like this. I should be having fun, not raising a child. God hurry get me out of here." She prayed for guidance.

The closer she got to the house the angrier her tears were. The deeper the depression took her. The faster she walked not realizing she held Tracy's hand, and Tracy was running behind her.

She was tired of taking care of Tracy. Yes, she loved her sister very much, but she wanted to have fun like other kids her own age. She just wanted to be a kid. She wanted to do what every twelve year old did. She wanted to be responsible for only herself.

How was she going to have a life, if she had to keep taking care of Tracy all the time? As she stood outside her house, she asked God to do something to change the mess that was her life. She also wondered if even God could do anything with this family. She went inside the house and fed Tracy, just as she did every day.

After Tracy fell, asleep Martha let the tears fall down her face into her pillow. She saw why she had to be the parent. She just wanted to live a normal life, go to the movies, and have friends over the house. This time she wished she could go to sleep and never wake up. However, she knew that Tracy would die too. There was no one to take care of her.

Every day she grew more tired. She would like one day off, even at her grandparent's house, she had to take care of Tracy. Martha was the only one Tracy felt safe around. Martha knew this feeling would pass, but she was still be tired of having to take care of Tracy all the time.

I have to stop thinking like this or I will make myself sick.

The tears poured out of her eyes and she buried her face in the pillow. She knew they could hear her crying. However, in this house no one cared. Everyone lived in his or her own world. Martha did not know how long or how hard she cried, but she finally fell asleep, and she was glad.

THE CURSE OF ALCOHOLISM

The years crept by. The drinking worsened. Genevieve's blackouts became more frequent. Genevieve disappeared for days at a time. Jose felt like the laughing stock of the town. He was the sheriff of Fair Lawn New Jersey for 15 years, and he was married to the town drunk. Jose tried to keep his parents from finding out about what he was going through with Genevieve. Martha was tired of the responsibilities put upon her by this dysfunctional family She couldn't even bring herself to invite friends over the house to play, because of her mom.

Tracy was glad when Genevieve did not come home for days. She had free run of the house. No more hiding in the park. However, Genevieve always came home again. Mad and yelling and looking for a drink. She kept unopened beer cans hidden throughout the house. Genevieve hid beer In between the stacked pots, under the sheets in the hall closet, in the drawers of the sewing machine table she never used. They were there for emergencies. When she had no money to go out and get more beer to drink, she cashed in Jose's Savings Bonds he had from the Navy. At other times, she cashed in the girls' silver dollars they got from the grandparents. She sold her clothes to consignment stores. She sold her jewelry and replaced it with custom jewelry. She would sell anything to get money to buy a drink.

One day, Genevieve staggered off drunk somewhere, and Jose was home from work sick. When the girls came home from school, Martha decided to make a pot of chicken soup. She heard that chicken soup help sick people get well. While Martha was making the soup in the kitchen, Tracy took a nap at the end of Jose's bed.

This could look like a normal family if someone looked in. No one saw the pain and sadness that lived behind the walls of this house. No mother nurtured here. There were no hugs and kisses at night. This was a house of torment.

The school placed Tracy in a Special Ed class. She learned slowly. She hardly spoke in school. The school called Jose in for a meeting to have him sign papers for Tracy to be placed in special Education. Martha warned Jose of the lie she had started in Tracy's first years of school. He was almost relieved that she had done that. However, he knew in his heart that in this small town some people knew the truth. Genevieve was the town drunk and not home bed ridden with polio.

A school bus picked Tracy in front of her house and took her to school. Tracy did not have to go to school with Martha. The bus brought her home a half hour after Martha got home.

Martha was in the ninth grade, and started earlier then Tracy. Tracy got home later then her. Still there were no friends for Martha. No staying for the football games after school. No going to friend's houses, or them coming to her house to hang out after school or weekends. Nothing changed; they were all prisoners to Genevieve's drinking problem. It became the whole family's problem. The family secret, the family sins, hidden behind the closed door.

Martha finished the soup and made a tray to take up to her stepdad's room. If Tracy was awake, Martha would see if she wanted to eat in her dad's room or in the kitchen. Martha gave Jose his tray he smiled and said, "Why don't you bring yourself and Tracy a bowl of soup, and we can watch TV together."

"OK, Dad, I'll get the TV guide and two trays, and we can just stay here with you." Martha smiled as she ran down stairs to get everything. This was the first time they had done anything together. She wanted her stepfather to love her. She wanted to be a family like on TV where the family eats together, and plays together. She pictured herself part of the Donna Reed family.

They were laughing at the Red Skeleton show, and they did not hear the front door open or the footsteps coming up the stairs. They did see Genevieve when walked into the bedroom. Everyone in that room took their eyes off the TV. They looked at Genevieve waiting to see what she would say or do.

She was drunk. Her hair and clothes were in disarray. Her lipstick smeared, her shoes wet from mud. They knew something was going to happen, and it was not going to be good. It seems like a long wait before she said anything.

Genevieve spoke in a slurred speech. "So, this is why you won't sleep in my bed you're having sex with my daughters," she said accusingly.

Martha wanted to take Tracy and run, but her mother was still holding on to the door facings. They could not leave they had to stay and hear the fighting. Jose got out of bed and walked towards Genevieve. There was so much anger on his face it scared the girls. They did not know what he was going to do. If looks could kill, she would have been dead.

When Jose got close to her, he slapped Genevieve across the face. "You sick drunk, take that back, or I'll beat the crap out of you, right here and now, in front of the girls."

Genevieve refused to take it back and Jose started to beat her. As soon as they were out of the doorway Martha took Tracy, ran to their room across the hall, locked it behind them.

Someone in the neighborhood called the police, because the noise from the fight was loud. Officers from Jose's station came to the house. They took both Jose and Genevieve to jail. No one knew the girls were home alone. No one asked if there was anyone else in the house. Martha was used to the fighting; it was part of the hell. Martha was able to block it out and go to sleep.

When Martha got up in the morning to go to school, she thought her dad went to work and her mother was down stairs sleeping off a drunk. She went about her morning just like any other morning. If the phone had not rang as she was leaving for school she would never have found out what had happened.

It was her dad," Martha, honey this is dad. I am on my way home; your mother and I spent the night in jail for domestic violence. I am so sorry I lost control last night. I just snapped. Can you forgive me?" He said with shame in his voice.

"Sure dad, I didn't hold it against you. Mom does that to people. See you when you get home". She said trying to comfort him. Martha did not understand that domestic violence was a crime, and not acceptable.

The drinking continued. The beating continued. Now they were fighting with each other, and Genevieve left Tracy alone. She did not even know she was around. It was winter. Sometimes it was too cold to go to the park with the snow on the ground. Now they came home and went to their dad room to watch TV Genevieve hardly climbed the stairs anymore, still they kept the bedroom door locked. The only one they opened it for was Jose. Then they would go across the hall and go to bed.

Was God concerned with this family and their problems? Was he ever going to change things for the good or was this their way of life. Was this going to be the norm for this family? Would they never be a family like the ones on TV?

WILL THIS EVER END?

Jose was fed up with the drinking. Three times, he got his wife out of the drunk tank at the county jail where he worked. Too many times to mention he was called to bars in different towns to pick up his wife who had passed out and left the girls alone in the parking lot unattended. Jose had told her it was her drinking or him. She knew she had nowhere to go. She also knew he would take her to court for custody of the girls.

She decided to call places for help. The waiting lists were six months long. Finally, she found a place that would take her. They wouldn't admit her until Friday. She had one week to drink for the last time. That is just what she did; Drink as if she was desperate to get it out of her system. Not knowing that an alcoholic cannot stop when they want to. The harder she drank, the less willing she was to believe she had a problem. She was just going there to shut Jose up.

On the way home from the liquor store on the Thursday before she was to be admitted to the hospital, she got so drunk she began hallucinating. Bugs were crawling up her arms and down her legs as she drove her 1956 powder blue Chevy two door. She saw ants trying to get in her car. They were all over her. Genevieve slammed on her breaks and started screaming so loudly that the school crossing guard came over to see what was wrong.

It was pouring rain that day and here came this man dressed in all yellow, yellow boot, yellow hat, yellow long rain coat the only thing that was not yellow was the red stop sing he had in his hand.

"Miss are you all right?" the crossing Guard, asked her while he knocked on the car window.

"Can't you see them all over the car, get back or the ants will get all over you," she said in terror.

16

"Miss there are no ants on your car or are there bugs on you inside the car" he told her. She screamed louder and louder until she passed out.

The crossing guard opened her car door and she fell out on to the street. By now, a group of people had gathered around to see what was going on. A woman holding a large red umbrella said "Oh that's that Diaz woman drunk again, something should be done with her." Just then the ambulance arrived.

Tracy was in the seventh grade when her mother caused the scene in front of her school. She stood by the window sharpening her pencil when she heard her mother's screams.

She saw her mother waving her hands in the car. Not really understanding what was going on she laughed. It was funny watching her mom throw her hands around and yelling something about bugs.

Tracy really laughed when Genevieve fell out of the car. Her laughter was inside; no one heard her laugh or saw the smile on her face when the paramedics put Genevieve in the ambulance. When the ambulance left Tracy returned to her seat like nothing had happened. The difference was Tracy continued to smile.

Her Teacher, Mrs. Larson noticed her smile, because she had never seen Tracy smile before. Mrs. Larson wondered what this meant after all these years. Miss Larson was the special ed teacher. She was a short black woman about five-foot-two. She had a short tight curly hair. She always wore dark skirts and blouses. She always smiled even when she was angry for something a student did. She wore moccasins for shoes. She was a little on the chubby side.

The time away from Genevieve was strange. Tracy could walk through the house without Genevieve doing or saying something to her. She started to change as the days turned into weeks and the weeks turned into months.

Tracy had spent six months away from Genevieve. For months, she had to remind herself Genevieve was not there. She would catch herself looking in closets for her. She still made the peanut butter, jelly sandwiches, and hid them in the bushes. For six months, she came home and got her sandwich, ate it then went into the house, ready to run back out if Genevieve was there.

Genevieve was in the hospital for three months suffering from hallucinations. Her head hurt from the shakes, and she wondered if it would ever stop. Her depression was so deep, and yet she could not die. She was in so much pain, but death never came. The nerve pills only helped some of the time. She had pills to bring her up and pills to help her sleep.

Genevieve now had depended on the pills to keep the bad feelings away. She passed from booze to drugs. The doctors told her she would have to be off drugs before she could go home.

Would she ever go home? All they wanted to do in group was remind her of the bad things she had done.

"How Was This Going To Help! " She yelled one-day in-group.

The AA meeting she had to go to twice a day depressed her also. All they wanted to talk about was why they were sorry. Whom they had to tell they were sorry to. Some seemed happy. Some seemed different than they were when she first met them. Some had not had a drink in months. She could not imagine not having a drink for months. The weeks were killing her, and she knew she was going to get a drink as soon as they let her out of this hellhole.

The desire to drink faded but never completely left her. As the weeks passed, she saw what all this had done to her family. Now, all she wanted to do was stop drinking, live a normal life, and stop making excuses. She faced the fact that she drank because she liked to drink. Drinking made her feel strong and important. The first taste was bitter but after a few drinks, it tasted sweet. Everything was funny and not important, as it was when she was sober.

Finally, the day came when Genevieve's family was to take her home from the hospital. She had been there six long hard months. Everyone was nervous, including Genevieve. She did not trust herself. She knew, if the need for a drink got too bad, she could pop some pills, and she would be O.K. Jose saw calmness in Genevieve that he had not seen since they were first together. Martha saw the mother she had before Genevieve started drinking.

She had been in the hospital for six months. She smiled as she rememberd her thoughts in the hospital. She no longer wanted to head for a bar, to get that drink. She was sober, clear headed, and calm. She knew she could never drink again. She knew she had to go to her meetings to stay sober. The difference now was she wanted to stay sober more then she wanted a drink. She knew that one drink and the nightmare would start all over again.

Tracy had not gone to see her mom even once the whole time she was in the hospital. Every time her dad and Martha went to visit, Tracy stayed in the lobby and waited. Tracy refused to see her mom, and her dad did not force her.

The medical staff told Genevieve and Jose not to force Tracy and to take it slow. From Genevieve's talks in meetings, they knew Genevieve had done a lot to Tracy, and it was going to take time for Tracy to trust her mother.

Today, like always, Tracy waited downstairs while her dad and Martha went upstairs to get Genevieve. The release took about one hour. Then the elevator doors opened, and the three walked off the elevator into the lobby. Tracy got up and followed behind them out the door of the hospital to the car.

They drove home in silence, all lost in their own thoughts. Jose was thinking he would give this marriage one more chance. He also hoped this was not just an act to get out of the hospital and back to the bottle again. Martha hoped they all could be like a family again. She knew it would take time. She had faith that she was finally going to have the family she wanted.

"God does answer prayer," Martha remembered the pastor saying. Tracy knew she had to stay out of Genevieve's way at all times. Tracy neither trusted nor liked Genevieve. She was glad Granddad was coming to pick her up tomorrow. Martha did not want to go her grandparents this year, she wanted to stay home and help her mom.

"Let her stay home, I don't care. Mother is just going to use her." Tracy told herself as they turned into the driveway of their house.

Tracy was glad she did not have to stay there and see the hell Genevieve was going to bring to this family again. She was going to start drinking as soon as their backs were turned. Genevieve was a drunk, and only she could stop the drinking. She was going to act as she was changed but Tracy knew she was going to drink again. How many times had Genevieve tried to stop drinking? How many times had she failed and looked for her booze again?

They were hoping for something that was never going to happen. She was going to break their hearts and disappoint them. Tracy was not going to be disappointed because she did not have false hope in Genevieve. She knew this was going to break their trust and she did not want to be here when it happened. She was so glad she was leaving in the morning. She was going to the house of love and peace where her grandparents lived.

She just wanted this night to be over so she could go to their house. She had plans for them. She was going to see the three movies she asked Martha to take her to but Martha did not have time with all the chores she had to do around the house.

She tried to help but Martha liked things perfect, and Tracy never did anything perfectly. Tracy would start many jobs and forget where she last was and she would leave them half done. This would make Martha mad and she would yell at her to go out and play. Tracy did not want to be grown up it was too much work. She did not have to work at her grandparents she just was there to have fun.

Her grandmother worked hard in the house. She did not have a washer or dryer she boiled her cloths early in the morning. She said machines do not wash good enough. She boiled, and strained her own coffee in the morning and baked her own bread. She made her own tortillas and they never ate sandwiches. Her grandmother was up with the sun and went to bed when the sun was down. She could not wait to get to that old fashioned family home. She loved them so much it was hard to fall asleep tonight knowing she was going there the next day.

Senen, (the girls grandfather), knew that the children suffered at his son Jose's house with that drunk for a mother. For years, he saw the embarrassment that she brought the family name. The Diaz name was a name respected in Spain. All Senen had in this country was his name. It was a name people knew and respected in New York.

That was why he asked the girls to spend the summer with them. He knew that Genevieve was torturing Tracy but he did not know what to do about it. He was here only on a visa, but he was not a citizen in this country. He did not know how the law worked. He also knew that someday he would not send Tracy home that she would chose to live there with them. He knew how much the girls love to go to grandma and grandpa house in New York. He lay in bed holding his wife in his arms knowing tomorrow Tracy was coming for the summer.

Semen's wife Tracy Sr. (Tracy was named after her), lay in bed next to her husband. She could feel how worried he was. He always held her tight the night before the girls came or the night before they left. She felt just as helpless as he did about the girls. It seemed that Tracy was getting better now that she was in school. She was spending less time around Genevieve. Tracy Sr. just could not figure out why Jose just did not leave Genevieve and take the girls when Genevieve went to the hospital. All she could do was love the girls. All she could do was make the summer fun for the girls, as she tried to do every summer. All she could do was fall asleep so she could rest for the summer with the girls..

SUMMER ALONE

This summer was different because Tracy had never spent a whole summer away from Martha before. She and her grandparents went to the movies every Saturday. Friday she went to the winery, which her granddad owned. They also went out to eat at lunchtime. In fact, it was even fun buying her school clothes. Everyone made it a point of not talking about her mom, but all good things must end. She remembered talking on the phone to Martha, she sounded calmer and less tense. Maybe it was because all Martha had to take care of was herself. That was alright with Tracy.

She hoped things were better for Martha. She remembered waking up at night when she was home, and hearing Martha crying. She wished she could do something for her but she could not even do for herself. She would just lay with her arm around her and say nothing. Sometimes that would make Martha cry harder. Tracy loved Martha so much and wished she did not have to depend on Martha so much.

Tomorrow night granddad would take Tracy home. Funny how it felt more like home here than it ever felt at her parents' house. Tracy could not help but wonder if her mom had started drinking again. She also wondered what it was going to be like at home.

She finally fell asleep. She no longer had to force herself to fall asleep. Now when she went to bed she fell asleep from tiredness. Tracy felt the Tiredness from having a good day with her grandparents. However, tonight it was her last night there. The night before the long drive home. To the house, she called home. What was a thirteen year old to do? She finally fell asleep.

Tension filled granddad's car as Tracy sat in the back seat. This was the first summer she went to her grandparent's house alone. Martha needed a break from Tracy so she stayed home with her parents. Martha never came right out and said it but everyone knew she needed the break. Tracy did not know what to expect from the family she was going home too. No one had said anything but she heard a difference in his or her voices when she called home. She heard laughter in their voices. A calmness that was never there before. Something was different.

As granddad pulled into the driveway, Martha came running out to meet the car. Oh, how Tracy loved her sister. After all, she took care of her. As they embraced, Tracy could see her parents coming out the door together.

Tracy had not known it but her mom, dad, and sister had been in counseling all summer while she was gone. There was Ala-non and ala-teen and AA meetings. They were beginning to heal from the nightmare without her.

Tracy was surprised to see her mother without a drink in her hand. Even more surprising to her was the fact that her father had his arm lovingly around her mother's shoulders. A cold chill ran over Tracy's skin as she walked silently past them into the house. She felt as if she was in an Outer Limits episode. She hoped her Grandfather would not leave for a long time. She did not want to be here alone for long. She was going to lock her bedroom door and put her bed against it for protection. She did not even trust Martha tonight. Martha never smiled before, but she was all smiles, hugs, and kisses tonight. Even Genevieve welcomed her home. Welcome? She was never welcomed here before.

Martha told Tracy that she would no longer sleep with her. Tracy would sleep in her old room down stairs across from mom and dad's room. That scared Tracy. Why was she put back so close to the woman who hurt her?

As she was shutting her bedroom door, she could see in her mother's room. She stopped long enough to see her father's PJ's at the foot of her mom's bed. She stopped in her footsteps to make sure what she was seeing was true. As she continued to look she also, saw her father's after-shave on what used to be her mother's empty dresser.

A pain shot, through her heart. "What's happening around here? Just having me out of here for a few months couldn't bring this much change." Tracy was afraid of what these changes would mean to her. She made up her mind to just stand back and watch.

Thank God, it was bedtime and school was starting in the morning. Sleep always helped shut out the hurt before, and she knew it would help now when she felt she needed it the most.

As she lay in bed, she heard her grandfather's car drive out of the driveway. This homecoming was confusing to Tracy. Why was everyone acting so happy? Were they all glad that they had a summer without her? Tracy was hurt that everyone was so happy. Why had they not done this while she was here? All these questions tormented her as she lay in her bed far away from Martha's room.

If she lay there long enough maybe, she would find the answers to her questions. Because sleep was not coming no matter how she tried to all asleep. Only the confusing questions kept her from resting. At least before, she knew what to expect. She was use to the old fears. This was scarier. This certainly was something out of the *Twilight Zone*.

Tears started to fall to her pillow. She knew that once she fell asleep she would find she had only dreamt this. In the morning, she would find herself still in her bed at her grandparents and she had not gone home yet.

THE GIFT OF SOBRIETY

At home, many things were different. Genevieve had not taken a drink in nine months. The first two months she went to AA meetings twice a day. In two weeks, she would have an anniversary party at the Alcoholics Anonymous club where Genevieve attended her meetings.

Sobriety was not an easy road, it was long and hard, and the battle would take a lifetime to control. Genevieve knew she had broken the power drinking had on her. She still wanted to drink, but her desire to stay sober was stronger. Genevieve was better able to face things now.

She found out why she drank. It was her way to cover up her fears. She also found out she was sick and this sickness prevents people from drinking ever again. She knew that if she ever took one drink it would start the nightmare all over again.

Hate and self-pity now longer controlled her actions. She slowly began to forgive herself for the way she treated Tracy. Genevieve could not dwell in the past. She must take one day at a time.

However, Genevieve wondered how Tracy would take the news that she was pregnant. Her relationship with Jose was getting better every day, but there was still a certain distrust between them.

Jose feared Genevieve wouldn't stay sober. She drank without anyone knowing before while she was pregnant with Tracy. He hated the fact that he could not trust her completely. After all, they had gone through with the drinking. He sure did not want to go back there.

Jose still was afraid to trust Genevieve completely. He moved his things back into the downstairs bedroom two months earlier. Every day when he came home, he expected Genevieve to be drunk. Since he still worked two jobs, he left before Genevieve woke up in the morning. When he came home at 3:30 p.m., Genevieve was there cooking dinner.

She never learned how to cook; but then again, that was not the reason he fell in love and married her. He always stopped to eat out before he came home. This way he only had to eat a little and not hurt her feelings. When he returned home from his second job at eleven thirty p.m., Genevieve was just coming home from her A. A. meeting. They would talk a little while, and then go to bed. As they lay in bed waiting for sleep to come, they were thinking of Tracy's coming home tomorrow. Now that summer was over Jose wondered what effect Tracy is coming home would have on Genevieve's drinking problem. Genevieve was wondering how she would start a relationship with Tracy. She knew she had done many hurtful things to Tracy. She knew she had never been a mother to Tracy. She wondered how she was going to transfer the love Tracy had for Martha to herself.

Meanwhile, Martha's life was changing fast, she was no longer Tracy's keeper; she was becoming a woman. Martha felt free from the torment of constantly worrying about her sister's safety. She had been able to come and go without worrying about Tracy's welfare. She did not even feel guilty for the peace inside herself. She loved Tracy but she was glad she had spent the summer without her. Jose had put a separate phone line in her bedroom. She was eighteen and needed her own phone, now that she had a boyfriend.

One week after Tracy went to her grandparents, Martha got a job at Planters' Peanut store downtown as a cashier. Now she was able to save money for things she needed. She bought her own clothes, and she bought herself a car. Jose co-signed for her and added her car to his car insurance.

Martha saved to buy a 1955 Chevy, powder blue, with cream color interior. Jose had tried to treat her like a daughter even though he was not her natural father. It is just that, while the drinking and fighting were going on, she did not feel the love.

She also met Roy, a tall, dark handsome German. He looked like Elvis Presley to her. At first, he was just a customer who came into her job for some peanuts, a half-hour before closing time. After about three months of going into the store, he asked her out on a date. They were dating every day, very much in love by the time summer was over, and Tracy was due home.

Martha knew when she finished school in June she and Roy would marry. Martha promised herself that her marriage to Roy would be better than her mom and dad's. She knew she would be a better mother to her children.

Martha knew that love did hurt sometimes, like when she and Roy had arguments, but making up always made being in love worth the pain. "Well, summer is over and Tracy will be home tomorrow night," she thought as she got ready for her date with Roy. She wondered how Tracy was going to handle all the changes at home.

Martha called Tracy every Sunday. They talked about home, and they never talked long. Martha never volunteered any information on the progress the family was making. She never told her about Roy.

Martha remembered how pale her mother was the day she gave her testimony at her AA meeting. It was so hard for Genevieve to tell all the things she had done to Tracy. No one realized all the pain Tracy had gone through.

Genevieve's sponsor Ellen said she broke down and cried a few times while she was telling her story. However, this was good therapy for Genevieve. It cleaned out the skeletons in her closet.

Sometimes we make mistakes and we hide them in our closets. However, we need to clean out the closets by forgiving ourselves so they don't torment us any longer. Give the things to God and turn out lives around. This way our slate is clean and people will soon see us differently.

Martha remembered how it was before Genevieve married her stepfather. She lived with her mother's mother and her step-grandfather. They were old very unhappy people.

Her grandmother, Virgie, was a short thin woman about five-foot-tall. She wore housedresses with flower prints on them. She had short curly light brown hair. She always had an apron on unless she was going out. Even if she was not cooking.

She was a simple cook. Not many spices in her food and not enough salt or pepper. She did not put them because she had high blood pressure. Her husband of thirty years was a quiet, gentle man who just listened to his wife without interjecting an opinion on any of the things she had to say.

He was a chubby man about five foot five in overalls and boots. They had chickens so he would go out every morning to get the eggs for Virgie. He was clean shaven, but his hair was not always combed. He had thin black hair. It was messy from the cap he wore whenever he went outside. It would separate in the back and it looked like he parted it with a comb. Hershel was not a man to smile but he never raised his voice in anger.

They never had a good thing to say about Genevieve. They always said she had been a disappointment to them. They never had anything good to say about their other children her siblings either. She was always scared to defend her mother because she was scared they would throw her out. They said Genevieve was living on the street and did not care about her or she would do something with herself.

Her mother told her they were lying when she called her on the phone each week. They talked about school and really nothing important. She would say she was coming for her as soon as she had something steady, whatever that meant. She never came to visit and Martha lived there for two long years. She did not really like it there but she stayed because her mother told her this was best for now. When Genevieve came for her, she thought it was going to be just the two of them. She was surprised and disappointed when on the train Genevieve told Martha she had gotten married. It was hard at first because Genevieve spent more time with Jose then with her. At least she was home and felt better then she had at her grandparents.

Now she was trying to live with the mother that had never been there for her. However, she was her mother. Drunk or sober this was the hand dealt to her and she had to make do. At least she could bring people over the house without worry her mother would come home drunk and make a scene. Life was going to get better for a change. She could go to bed worry free. For two months, all she had to do was take care of her.

WAS THIS REALLY TRACY'S FAMILY OR A DREAM?

Three months had passed since Tracy came home. Things were different, so different that Tracy did not know how to act at times. Genevieve never drank anymore, she never got crazy, and she never hit or threw Tracy in the closet. Genevieve was having another baby. No matter what Tracy did, and Tracy did try to push her mother with words of hate or defiance, her mother would simply say "Wait till your dad comes home, I'm going to have him deal with you."

Genevieve was scared to discipline Tracy. She was sure she would get out of control or hurt her. Whatever Tracy did was reported at the dinner table. This had also changed because now everyone ate together at the kitchen table. They now said Grace for the food before they ate. They talked and laughed as they ate. The days her mother told her dad of her defiance, her dad would just tell her she could not have dessert, and she had to go to her room. There was a different tone of voice, and a different feeling in their home now, but Tracy knew it would not last long. She knew the real family she knew would return. She knew these people in this house were not her family they were someone else in their bodies.

Tracy knew in her heart that it was a matter of time before her mom started drinking again. She still felt her parents did not love her. As soon as her mom had her baby in May, things would go back to the way they always were. The drinking started and the abuse would be directed towards the new baby. Genevieve would start drinking, her dad would move back upstairs, and poor Martha would have to take care of the new baby.

"Poor Martha will have to quit her job at Planters Peanuts, her new 1955 Chevy would have to go back to the car lot, and she would have no more time for Roy." Tracy smiled at these thoughts.

Tracy would not mind this. She was jealous of them being together every day anyway. Ever since Martha met Roy, Martha never had time for her anymore. Roy was a tall man over six foot. He looked like Elvis Presley to her. He even combed his hair like Elvis with that roll up curl in the front. His hands always looked dirty because he worked on carsm and the grease never came off completely. But he was good looking and always dressed nice.

If she was not going for rides with him, she was on the phone with him for hours. Tracy even told them lies about each other to try to break them up but no one believed her. In addition, they did not break up.

Roy stopped at the house every morning before going to work. He was back again every night. On the nights Genevieve had gone to her AA meetings, Roy came to dinner. For some strange reason, he felt he had to help Martha baby-sit and Tracy resented him.

Sundays he went to church with the family. What bothered Tracy most was when he came with them to her grandparent's house. Tracy's grandparents were getting old so her mom and dad drove her there on Fridays, and the whole family picked her up on Sundays.

Now that Roy was in the picture, her grandparents would speak their broken English. Tracy did not like this. This was supposed to be her special place. Now everyone was going there. This upset Tracy.

What right do they have to come to my grandparent's house. This is for me not them, only me.

Nothing was the same any more Tracy did not understand why everything was changing, before she knew what to expect. Now, she was scared and did not know why everyone loved everyone else and not her. Hate rose up in Tracy. She was turning bitter. She was going to keep the new baby for herself as Martha kept her. She was determined to hurt her mom the way Genevieve had hurt her. People needed to pay for the things they did. Why was she being rewarded? Why did God give her family to the woman that hurt her most?

When Genevieve bought anything for the baby, Tracy would steal it and hide it in her room. She would pile things in the hall closet. These things worried Jose and Genevieve. His was not a normal way for a girl of fourteen to act.

During Genevieves pregnancy, Jose decided to take Tracy to see a therapist because she was acting strange;y ever since she found out a baby was on the way. The school recommended Mrs. March. She dealt with many children of abuse.

A NEW BABY

In May, Genevieve and Jose had a baby girl; they named her Lisa. She was a small baby 5 lbs. 11 oz. She was only 19 inches long with no hair on her head. According to Tracy, Sr., she looked like Jose when he was a baby. When everyone went to the nursery window to see the new baby, they did not go in to Genevieve's room to visit her they just went to the nursery to see the new baby through the window.

The day they brought her home from the hospital, Tracy did not go, because she had to go see Mrs. March, her psychologist. When Tracy first started seeing her, she did not trust her. She thought she was a spy, and that she would report everything she said back to her mom.

Therefore, Tracy would make up things to make her Mom look bad to see if her mom would mention them to her dad at the dinner table. However, nothing was ever said, so she began to trust Mrs. March.

"Maybe she is trying to help me," she thought. Now when Mrs. March would ask her questions and Tracy would answer honestly. She asked Tracy to show her with the dolls she had how different members of the family acted towards each other. She portrayed Martha as loving and kind, and then she would show the Tracy doll as being good and nice to the Martha doll. Her mother she showed as hateful and drunk, she was yelling and always trying to hurt the Tracy doll. The Tracy doll would show bitterness and hatred towards its mother.

The father doll she showed as going to work all the time. Her feelings for her dad were sad, sad because she saw him only as a stranger. She knew nothing about him. He was the man that worked two jobs and pretended to laugh at the dinner table. It was the bitterness for her mother that worried Mrs. March. Tracy told her about the things she did to her mother that worried Mrs. March. Tracy enjoyed upsetting her mother; she felt the tables were, turned and she had a short time to hurt her mother before her mother started drinking and hurting her again.

After six months, Mrs. March felt Tracy needed to see her twice a week instead of only once. There was a lot of damage to repair before someone got hurt. She was scared Tracy might do something to Genevieve or the baby. Tracy talked about hiding somewhere with the baby so she would be her baby. She wanted to take care of Lisa as Martha had taken care of her.

Lisa slept in Tracy's old room, and Tracy moved her things upstairs to the room her dad used to sleep in. Tracy spent most of her time with her baby sister. She could not wait to get home after school to play with her new baby sister. She would change her diaper, and carry her around the house. When the weather warmed up, she would take her for strolls outside in her carriage. Tracy talked to Lisa as if she was her baby and not her little sister.

Sometimes she would tell her things like, "I'll take care of you when mom starts drinking again; she'll never hurt you like she did me."

She did not care who heard her say this. Since Tracy had Lisa, it did not bother her so much anymore that Martha had Roy.

Tracy began to make plans to take Lisa and go away. She saved every penny from her allowance. She was going to take her away from the bad people who would hurt her someday.

It was only a matter of time before all hell broke loose. This was her plan she would run away to another town and or maybe she would go to granddads and hide in the down stairs apartment.

She made a list of what she would need. Diapers, milk, bottles, change of clothes and things for herself. She would put it all in her backpack and take the stroller instead of the carriage. She would take the bus to the Brooklyn Bridge, and then she would take the Subway to her grandparent's house. The whole trip would take three or four hours. She would need two dollars for the bus and one dollar for the subway.

It only took one month to have all she would need for the trip. She told her mother she was going to the park to read while Lisa played. She had everything in her backpack.

As she was going out the door, Genevieve said, "Why don't you just go by yourself and leave Lisa here. It's ten in the morning and I could put her down for her morning nap." Tracy stopped by the door and tried to act as if it did not matter.

"I could just wait till after her nap, you know how she loves to play in the sand," Tracy said with no emotion in her voice to keep her mom from catching on. She decided it was now or after the nap but she was going today. Without another word, she left with Lisa in the stroller.

Somewhere in the back of Genevieve's mind, she heard a small voice say, "You better go to the park because I think Tracy has left with Lisa." With that, she got in her car and drove to the park. She drove around looking for Tracy and saw no one who even looked familiar.

With that, she drove back to the house and called Dr. March. Dr. March went over her notes to try to find out where Tracy would go. Finally, she found the page where she had asked Tracy what she would do if she were Lisa mother. With that, she drove to the bus station to try to find Tracy. When she arrived, she saw Tracy through the picture window sitting waiting for her bus. As Dr. March Walked towards her Tracy was putting money in the little TV that you put quarters in for a few minutes of TV.

Dr. March sat next to Tracy like nothing was wrong.

"What are you doing here, Tracy", Dr. March asked as she picked up the magazine that was lying on the seat next to her.

"Oh, Hi I'm going on a trip with Lisa. I have decided to raise her as my baby. After all I can take better care of her than her mother." Tracy thought nothing of Dr. March being there. After all, she had always popped up when things got difficult. She was there all the time so this was not different. This did not upset or cause Tracy to fear why she was there.

They talked for about 45 minutes. Dr. March Told Tracy she could go to jail for kidnapping Lisa, and then she would never see or protect her. She told her that if they went back home everything would be fine, and Tracy could still take care of Lisa. Dr. March told Tracy that if Genevieve started drinking even one drink, Tracy could call her and they would take the baby somewhere safe. Tracy finally agreed, and Dr. March drove them back to the house. Tracy promised never to take Lisa again without calling Dr. March first.

When they got to the house Tracy took Lisa in the house to put her down for her nap while Dr. March stayed outside with Genevieve and talked. They were afraid that this would happen again.

She was scared to trust Tracy alone with Lisa. Dr. March assured Genevieve this would never happen again. However, she did not tell her why she was so sure. She did not tell her that Tracy would call if Genevieve started drinking again. She only told her what she could. The rest of the conversation was confidential. At least the baby was home in just a few. Tracy still had many issues to work on.

DEATH BRINGS FEAR

When Lisa turned one year old, the family gave her a birthday party on Saturday. Tracy had never had a birthday party, but she was not jealous. She was having fun blowing up balloons and putting up streamers. Just decorating the living room was fun. Most of the kids who came were friends from AA. Tracy was finding out there were many kids with a parent who was an alcoholic.

She thought only her mother who drank. With Al-anon and Mental Health, Tracy's feelings for her mother were changing from hate to acceptance. Tracy even started liking Roy. She was talking more. Most important, she was starting to care about herself and others. The therapy was working. She was no longer a threat to anyone. She still had to see the doctor once a week.

There was only one more week before school would be out, then it would be time to go to her grandparents for the summer. This time she was going to work for her grandfather in the winery.

For the first time Tracy was not excited. The thought of leaving her baby sister was tough on her. She thought about telling her grandparents she only wanted to go on weekends, but she never had to make that decision.

Wednesday night her father got a phone call to go to the hospital. His mother had suffered a massive stroke, and the family was asked to come quickly. She was not expected to last the night.

Tracy knew nothing; she just thought her dad was at his night job. Who would tell Tracy? Who should they call to help Tracy through this? Thursday morning Tracy did not notice her dad was not home yet. She did notice how tired her mother looked, but she just thought the baby had kept her awake again. This was the day of the party at school, the last day of the year, and she hurried this morning, but it finally came and Tracy left.

School was fun. She now had friends, and they signed her T-shirt. They only had half a day at school so she went home early. She no longer took the bus home. She was no longer in special Ed. They called it mainstreaming. Putting them in with children that were normal. She was running home singing. She was going to take Lisa to the park to swing on the swings.

Lisa loved the swings. She would scream with laughter, "Push me sissy, and push me faster." Tracy loved taking her to the park.

As Tracy got closer to the house she saw a lot of cars. "What if something had happen to Lisa," she said to herself.

She ran as fast as she could to see what happened, dropping her lunch box and all her papers from school. When she entered the house, she saw her grandfather sitting, looking out the window with tears running down his cheeks. His face told that something awful had happened.

She looked to the other side of the living room and she saw her aunt comforting her Uncle. She never saw them unless they went to her grandparents' house.

Why are they here?

It could not be Lisa. She was asleep on the mat by the hallway entrance. If she were sick or something, she would be in the hospital. Maybe it was her dad, maybe he got sick again, and no one noticed her as she walked into the kitchen. As she stood by the door, she could see her mom and sister at the kitchen table. Her Dad's face was on the table lying in his hands. His shoulders shook from crying. She was scared now. She did not understand what was happening. As she was about to ask questions the doorbell rang. It was Dr. March. Someone called her to tell Tracy the news.

She told Tracy to sit at the table. She needed to tell her something important. Tracy listened to the words, but it was as she was not there. As if Tracy had left her body, and she was far away from the hurt and pain, that she felt for years, everything turned black and the voices were gone.

She felt that tears were running down her face. She saw the family come into the kitchen. She saw her mouth open as if to scream. However, she heard nothing. After a few minutes, everything went black. The voices were gone; all the people in the kitchen were gone. The pain went away. If only she could stay there forever.

She could hear someone screaming "No, stop, don't say anymore, it's not true, you're lying." She didn't know who that was.

How was she going to live when the only people that loved her were dying? This woman would sit her on her lap, hold her, and sing songs in her ear. This was the first woman she had trusted with her love. Now she was gone. Life would not be the same. It would be some kind of pain in her life every day.

This was harder on Tracy than the abuse she had suffered from her mother. Would she ever get over this? Was this what was going to cause her to lose her mind?

DEATH BRINGS GREED

Grandmother had been dead a month now, and it still hurt. Tracy thought she would never get through her death. The whole family suffered from her death, but Tracy took it hardest.

Grandmother's house was a refuge from everything. There was no tension, no anger only love. Now where was she going to go when mom starts drinking again? Tracy would not believe that her mother was not going to drink again. Even at the funeral, she watched her mom expecting her to drink. When she left the room, Tracy followed her to see if she was going to get a drink. However, she did not take a drink.

Her grandfather went to stay with his other son. This way he could be closer to the winery. However, grandfather had not gone to work since grandmother died. All he did was sit in a chair and cry. Everyone knew it would not be long before he, too, died.

He would tell people he did not want to live. He always told Tracy "If you love me you would help me die."

She would answer him," I love you and I want you here with me." Then she would give him a kiss and a hug. He was not eating like he use to and each time Tracy hugged him she felt less skin and more bone. He was wasting away with grief and he just wanted to be away from the pain in his heart.

Jose had finally gone back to work after taking his two weeks' vacation. He had called his job and asked for the time off because his mother had died.

Those weeks after the funeral he spent in the basement. He had his tools down there and a workbench. Taking a hammer and nailing something into wood relaxed him. After two weeks, he came up with a big dollhouse for Tracy and a jewelry box for Martha. He also made a curio cabinet for Genevieve and he fixed Tracy's old tricycle for Lisa.

It was so hard for a man to lose his mom. She had been the one he went to when he needed something. He loved his father, but they were not close. His father did not know how to hug or give words of encouragement. He always expected more than Jose could offer. He knew his father loved him, but he was still closer to his mother.

The rest of the family dealt with the death in their own way. However, death also had become a reality to the family now. Before now, no one expected any one to die. People think they will live forever when they are young. They think they will always be there. Now, they start looking at people differently. They worry when they are sick, or if they are late coming home, or their call is late. They think of death most of the time. They wonder if they will die soon. They wonder how they will die. And when will it happen?

Death took Tracy's mind off her vendetta towards her mom. Now when she went to see Dr. March all she talked about was death and dying. She asked her about the people in her family that died. How they died. How old they were when they died. Every week Dr. March would try to change the subject. However, Tracy only wanted to talk death. She told Dr. March that she hated grandmother's sisters and that they were greedy

Her grandmother's sisters had gone to the house to ask Jose what his dad was going to do with their sister's things. Tracy got mad. She felt all that grandmother had belonged to them not her sisters.

Jose told his aunts it was up to his dad what happened to his mother's things. They got mad and left.

How could they be so cold blooded, and greedy? Tracy thought. Did they even care about her grandmother?

She wanted to board up the house so no one could get in. However, her dad thought that was ridiculous.

All this was too much for Tracy and all the anger and hurt and fears from the past took over her again. Tracy started screaming in her room and could not stop until she blacked out.

Jose called Mrs. March, and she said she would send an ambulance for Tracy. They took her to Bergen Pines hospital where she spent five months sorting things out. She was on antidepressants. She was in a locked facility where the meals were served in the room you slept in. She was required to go to therapy twice a day. She was feeling like she was in the closet again, and Martha would not open the door. She was released for the funeral and went right back to the hospital until she became an outpatient

DEATH STIKES AGAIN

This year the family went to visit dad's brother every Sunday. Their grandfather still lived there with them. Tracy did not like the way her cousins were all over him. After all that was her grandfather. Grandfather did not love them the way he loved her so it only bothered her little.

When they went there, she would sit next to him and speak in Spanish. She reminded him of the summers they spent together. This saddened him and made him think of his wife.

She would remind him of the secret password. "*Te quiero con todo mi Corazon*", I love you with all my heart. She reminded him of the song they sang together "*Usta la gusto, usta la gusta eah.*" They would sing faster and faster until they would get tongue-tied and start laughing.

However, all he would do was smile and look back out the window. Now he did not join in the password. Now he did not join in the singing. Now he no longer cared.

One day her uncle came to the house to say Granddad was selling the winery. He said they needed to meet with a lawyer to do the paper work.

Uncle Juan said, "Dad wants to keep the name Diaz wine on the labels. He wants to sell the winery not the name. He will not sell unless the name stays. He does not want to go to work anymore. I think he's giving up on life and wants to go be with mom."

There were tears in Jose's eyes as he nodded his head in agreement. However, it was true, ever since his wife died, he had lost his will to live. Now, he looked like a little man. All his life had been a big man. Now he was empty and did not care about anything.

Granddad did not smile or laugh any more. It was as if he wanted to die and was mad each day he woke up and was still alive. It was now a dreaded time when they would go to granddads and Uncle Abel's house. It was so heavy with depression over at their house.

Tracy use to think that if he had lived with her things would have been different. However, not anymore, Tracy knew his will left when Grandmother died, and he just wanted to be with her. Tracy was going to miss him when he died but it was going to be better for him. It was hard on everyone seeing him like that, all down and depressed. They all knew it was not going to be long. They had to force him to eat. He always said he was not hungry. Tracy could not remember a day when she was not hungry. Even when she was sick, she wanted to eat. All they could do is waiting for him to die. It was sad but true.

One year to the day grandfather died. He had not come down for breakfast so aunt Louise stayed home from work. She was worried about him. Because it was the anniversary of his wife's death, he wanted to die. By lunchtime, she was worried when he had not come down stairs at all.

She slowly went up and knocked on his bedroom door. No one answered. She knocked a few more times before opening the door. There he was still in bed. With a smile on his face, as if he knew he was with his wife that died. As she walked slowly towards him she softly called his name," Dad wake up are you ready for lunch". In her heart, she knew he was gone. She touched his cold face with her cheek, it was cold against hers, and she knew he was dead. She turned and went to call the Paramedics and her husband to let them know his father was dead.

This funeral was easier than the other was. Everyone knew he wanted to be with his wife. It had been hard to watch this man get old and drawn so fast. Juan remembered him in the eulogy he gave. He talked about the man that raised him in Spain. He was strong and you feared and respected him. When he told you to do something, you did it. There was hardly any time for play.

First school then the grapes. That was the way it was when he was growing up. It was that way seven days a week. No days off. Just school and work in the grapes.

"Dad always said, no works no eat. If you want something work for it," Juan told them. "He was a hard man, but a soft grandfather. He lived for his grandchildren. They had him wrapped around their little fingers." He said as he winked to his sons. The tears still came down but not like when his mother died unexpectedly.

People die for different reasons at different times in their lives. The families are the ones who must pick up the pieces and go on. Once the funeral is over, they have to work on getting on with their lives. This is the time people either get closer to God or curse him and walk away. It either brings families closer together or drives them farther apart. Only time can tell what Grandfathers death will do to this family.

This family never did what was expected of them. Most of the time it did what was not expected at all. This was why things were brought to the extreme. What was normal for this family, even in death, was pain.

Death will bring a family closer or farther apart. In this case, it drove a wedge between them.

The story continues in Book Two to be released Spring 2014